MAKE ME A ZOO

Creative Art Projects For PreK – 3

by Dorothy Cowan

Incentive Publications, Inc.
Nashville, Tennessee

Cover and illustrations by Jan Hoffman
Edited by Sherri Y. Lewis

ISBN 0-86530-177-8

Table of Contents

INTRODUCTION

If you have been searching for quick and easy creative art projects to capture and hold your students' attention, this book just may mean that your search has come to an end.

As students complete these easy-to-make pretzel owls, egg carton dragons, lunch bag deer, and other creative projects, they will enjoy a sense of artistic achievement without even realizing that "learning, too" is taking place. Equally important is the fun and excitement sure to be generated by ownership of these imaginative animals.

The activity plans include a linking of readily obtainable materials, concise and easy-to-follow instructions for project completion as well as accompanying illustrations for visual reinforcement.

A bonus collection of animal patterns is also included for use with the activities in the book or as inspiration for additional teacher and student generated projects.

The purpose of MAKE ME A ZOO is to encourage individual creativity and add sparkle and zest to daily classroom routines.

STRING PAINTING

Materials Needed

- One precut zebra shape of white paper for each child (See pattern on page 56.)
- Black paint in a pan or wide-mouthed container
- A 10" to 14" length of wide yarn or other wide string
- A brush
- Newspaper or other table protector

Lay the zebra shape on newspaper to keep paint off the table.

Holding one end of the yarn, push the rest into a pan or wide-mouthed jar of black paint using a brush, if needed, to push it down. Lift the yarn out of the container and drag the paint-covered part repeatedly across the zebra shape to form stripes. Redip the yarn as needed.

You can encourage the children to put stripes on all parts of the zebra, but stop them before the whole zebra is black.

Other shapes to try: tiger, cat, snake.

INK BLOT INSECTS

Materials Needed

- One sheet of paper per insect in white or a light color
- Ink or black tempera paint (The latter is easier to clean up and get out of clothes.)
- Paintbrush or eyedropper
- Newspaper to protect the surface
- Black crayon, felt-tip marker, or scraps of paper (optional)

Have the children fold their paper in half by matching edges and corners and creasing. If they don't match exactly, you can still get the insect – it just has a different position.

Unfold the paper and lay on newspapers. Drop ink or paint onto paper with a brush or eyedropper. Refold paper on crease. Rub the paper in all directions from the fold. Open the paper and give your insect a name – if you can.

When the painting is dry, you may let the children add eyes, antennae, or more legs using crayons, felt-tip markers, or glued-on shapes using cut or torn colors from the scrap box.

PET CAGES

If needed, cut out the animal to be put in a cage. Fold the paper for the front of the cage in half lengthwise. Cut from the fold to within 1 inch of the edge. If children are very young, prefold the paper and draw a line 1 inch from the open edge and parallel to the fold. Have the children cut to the line. Open the paper flat. Leaving the outside strips, cut out alternate strips where they are attached near the open edge. Unfold, and you have the cage. Glue the animal to the background paper. Place the cage you cut over the animal, gluing securely around the outside edges. If the edges don't quite match, trim off the background paper until the edges are even.

You can add a handle for carrying by using one of the strips cut off from the cage. Or, you can make a yarn handle.

Punch two holes about 4 inches apart near the middle at the top of the cage. Make a knot in one end of the yarn and put the other end through both holes. Make another knot in the unknotted end of the yarn and you have a hanger.

BUTTERFLY PRETZELS

Materials Needed

- A picture of grass and trees or flowers painted by the child or cut from a magazine
- One straight pretzel and two knotted pretzels for each butterfly
- Glue
- Stiff backing
- Crayon – probably black (optional)

Staple or glue the dry painting or picture to the background (stiff backing).

Place glue on one side of a straight pretzel and place on the background paper. Put glue on one side of a knotted pretzel and lay it on the paper next to a long side of the straight pretzel. Repeat with the other pretzel placing it on the other side of the straight pretzel.

Add as many butterflies as is appropriate to the size of the paper or the time allowed.

SPONGE-PAINTED BAT

Materials Needed

- A precut bat shape of white or manila paper cut from 12" x 18" paper (See pattern on page 60.)
- Small sponges – which can be held with spring clothespins for neater hands
- Shallow pans of black or brown tempera paint

Place the bat shape on a protected surface.

The children place a sponge in the paint and then press it gently on the bat shape. They lift it and press in another spot until more paint is needed. The children get more paint on the sponge and repeat the procedure until the bat is painted as much as desired.

Discourage smearing as with a brush or pressing so hard that runny paint comes out of the sponge.

FISH

Materials Needed

- Triangles in two sizes in a selection of colors
- Precut (or let children cut) circles in a variety of sizes and colors
- A background for the fish
- Glue or paste

- Scissors (optional)

Each child selects a large and small triangle.

He/she puts some glue under the right angle point of the small triangle and glues it to the center of the long side of the large triangle.

He/she selects or cuts circles and glues them to the fish for its markings.

Then he/she glues the fish to the background paper. This can be a blue, a green, or a blue and green fingerpainting. You can add some sand to the fingerpaints when you mix them to add texture and another sensory experience.

Or, you can use blue and/or green paint to brayer-paint a mural size paper; then everyone puts their fish (properly marked with names on the back) in the ocean. (Or cut construction paper in a color you or the children choose.)

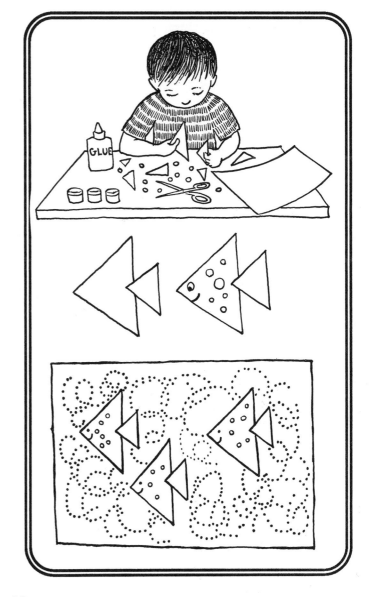

ANIMAL-SHAPED PRINTING SPONGES

Materials Needed

- Animal shapes cut from sponges
- Paper on which to paint – place mats for a party, a dried fingerpainting, newsprint, or construction paper
- A pan of water to dampen the sponge
- Tempera paint in shallow pans – one color or several choices

Place the paper to be painted on a protected surface.

Use soft sponges or old foam pillows or cushion forms for the animal shapes. Using 3/4" to 1" thickness of sponge, cut an animal shape with scissors – a sitting cat, rabbit, turtle, fish, dinosaur, dolphin, snail, etc., something without too many appendages.

Cut a slit in the back of the sponge so a craft stick can be inserted about an inch. Put glue in the slot and insert the stick. Press sponge and the stick together. Let the glue dry, and you have a handle for the sponge.

Dampen the sponge in the water. Squeeze out excess water.

Place one side of the sponge in a shallow pan of paint.

Place the sponge on the paper where you want a print and press down lightly. One dip in the paint will make more than one print. Redip as needed for more prints.

When finished, wash your sponge shape and save for many years of use.

BABY CHICKS

Materials Needed

- One large and one small yellow circle for each baby chick
- One sheet of background paper per child
- Crayons or felt-tip markers
- Glue or paste

The children paste the large circle on the background paper for the body of the chick. Then the small circle is added for the head of the chick making a slight overlap of the circles where they meet.

Use crayons or felt-tip markers to draw an eye (or two), a beak, and two legs with toes that make the chicken's feet.

Several chicks can be put on the same paper as a group. This can also be the front of an Easter card.

SUNSET HORSE SCENE

Materials Needed

- Watercolors
- White paper for watercoloring (9" x 12" or larger)
- Containers of water to wash brushes
- Black construction paper
- A horse shape cookie cutter to use as a template
- Scissors
- Glue

Place watercolors, water container, and white paper on a protected surface.

Use the paintbrush to drop two drops of water on each color pan to be used – blue, yellow, orange, red, green, and/or brown. Wet the white paper with a sponge or dip it in a pan of water.

Paint a sunset scene by painting a band of blue across the top of the paper.

Wash the brush in water by "painting" the bottom of the water jar between each color use.

Paint a yellow strip across the paper next to the blue strip, followed by orange, red, brown, and green in widths that will have the paper covered by the last one – green. Widths can vary.

Let the paint dry. Clean up the brushes and paints.

Use the horse-shaped cookie cutter and template to draw a horse on the black paper. Use a white crayon or chalk if you feel a pencil line will be too hard to see. The chalk or paper may have to be dampened to get a good line for cutting.

Cut out the horse or horses.

Glue the horse or horses to the dry watercolor painting. If you don't want flying horses, you may need to point out that some of the horses' feet should be on the green or the brown.

Optional: For older children, the horses could be done with watercolor or felt-tip markers.

When the original watercolor is dry, wet only the black watercolor pan. When the pan is ready, put black paint on the brush. Have the child paint an upside-down "V."

Put more black paint on the brush and make a horizontal line from one of the bottom "V" points.

Get more black paint on the brush and add an upside-down "V" near each end of the horizontal line.

With another batch of black paint, make a slanted down line from the tail end of the horizontal line. They can make more than one horse in this manner.

Let the paintings dry before moving them.

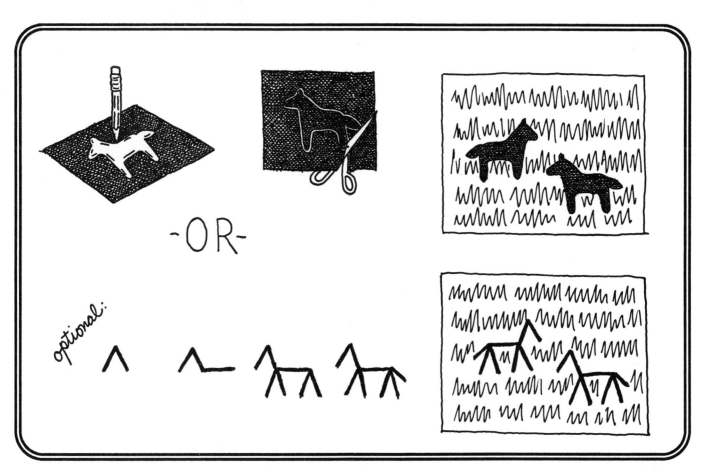

RESTING BLACK CATS

Materials Needed

- One 9" x 12" or 12" x 18" sheet of construction paper
- Scraps of yellow or green construction paper
- Glue or paste
- A large sheet of paper (optional – to mount the cat)
- Scissors

Fold the sheet of construction paper in half lengthwise. Open the sheet. Using the fold line as a guide, cut a large semicircle from one of the halves. Starting at one corner, cut a large curve up to the fold and down to the other corner.

From the scraps of that half, cut a curved tail and four straight, thin pieces for whiskers.

From the other half of the paper, cut a large circle for the head and two relatively small triangles for the ears.

Cut a nose, two eyes, and a mouth (if desired), from the colored scraps.

Glue the eyes and nose (and mouth) on the circle that is the head. Cut two black slits (ovals) and glue vertically in the eyes.

Glue the two triangles to the top of the circle for the ears.

Glue the head to one end of the curve that is the body.

Glue the tail to the other end.

THE CEREAL BEAR

Materials Needed

- One sheet of construction paper (no brown)
- A template or predrawn bear shape
- Pencil (optional)
- Glue

- Quantities of nature-type cereals, crushed wheat, or crushed brown cereal flakes
- Two black-eyed peas for each bear
- One brown bean for each bear

If the bear shape is not predrawn, place the template in the middle of the paper and draw around the bear.

It is better if you staple or securely glue the construction paper to the same size cardboard for a backing (one backed sheet per child).

Cover the bear shape with glue. (Placing globs of glue on the bear shape and spreading with a finger is most successful for a full coverage.)

Wash and dry hands thoroughly.

Sprinkle cereal over the glue-covered area, hiding the glue.

Use the palm of the hand flat to gently press the cereal into the glue.

Use two black-eyed peas for the eyes, pushing them through the cereal to the glue.

Press in one brown bean below the eyes for a nose.

Allow to dry thoroughly before much or any movement of the picture.

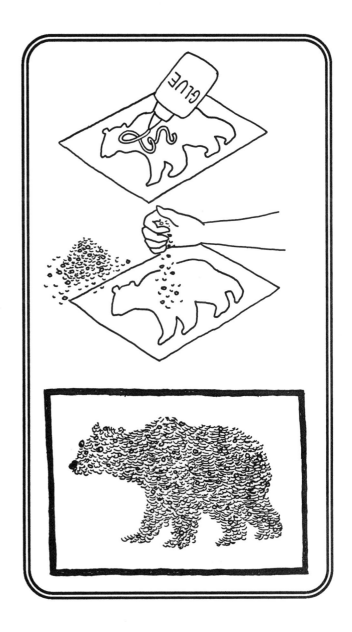

A VALENTINE ELEPHANT

Materials Needed

- Two precut or predrawn same-size pink hearts per elephant
- A 1 inch wide pink strip (trunk)
- Scissors
- Paste or glue
- Scraps of construction paper (to cut eyes)
- A pencil
- If you wish to mount the elephant on a sheet of paper or the front of a valentine card, supply one per child.

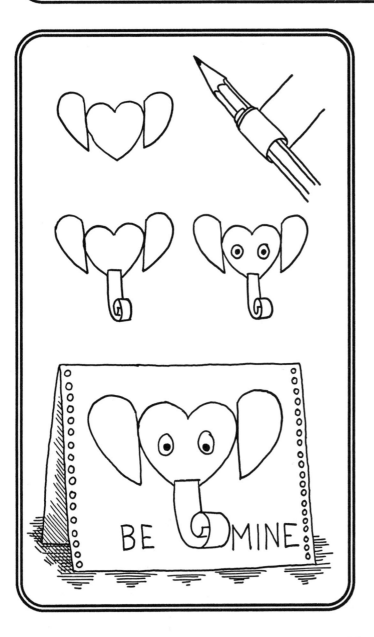

Cut out the valentines if not already cut.

Cut one valentine in half. Glue a half to each side of the other valentine for ears. The ears should extend above the head, and the points should extend a bit to the side of the lower part of the valentine.

Roll at least half the pink strip around a pencil to curl one end.

Glue the uncurled end to the bottom of the valentine for the trunk. (Trunk length should be in relation to the size of the ears.)

Cut or tear two eyes from scraps of paper and glue them in place. Add two smaller shapes to the eyes for pupils.

Glue the animal head to the front of a card or a sheet of paper if desired, or display as is.

If used as a valentine, messages can be added.

BIRDS

Materials Needed

- 9" x 12" or 12" x 18" construction paper (one sheet per child)
- Feathers
- Yarn or fat string
- Glue
- Bird seed (optional)

Use feathers to create a bird. Glue the feathers to the construction paper.

Use string or yarn (bird cage length per paper size – 4 or 5 lengths per child) to make the bird cage by putting glue on each end of a piece of string and laying it vertically over and near the bird, pressing down the ends firmly. Add a horizontal string to the top and bottom of the cage if it seems visually needed.

Add some bird seed for the bird to eat by putting some glue on the bottom of the cage and pressing some bird seed into it.

Let the picture dry before trying to move it.

WATER-PAINTED BUTTERFLIES AND MOTHS

Materials Needed

- A sheet of white 9" x 12" paper for watercolors (one per butterfly)
- A 9" x 12" sheet of colored construction paper*
- Watercolors
- Watercolor brushes
- Water containers for washing brushes
- Pencil if template is used
- Scissors
- Glue or stapler
- Sponge and water
- Brown or black crayon or marker

Place watercolors, containers of water, brushes, and white paper on a protected surface.

Wet all pans of watercolors you expect to use – all colors can be used in moderation. Brown and black can muddy up the scene, but there are brown and black butterflies and moths.

With a very wet sponge, wet the white paper on one side. Even small puddles of water are acceptable.

Dip a wet brush into a color pan; then touch it to the wet paper. Do not use painting strokes. Let the water spread the color. Touch the paper in other places until the bead of paint is used and little color is deposited.

Wash the brush by "painting" the bottom of the water jar. Rub the brush against the edge of the jar and reload the brush with more color – the same or different – and touch the paper in other places. Repeat until the paper is as colorful as wanted, but make sure the children stop before it turns to muddy water.

Let the painting dry.

*Use blue for sky, green for grass, brown for mud, etc.

If the butterfly shape is not already drawn, fold the piece of colored paper in half – either way. Use a template to draw half of a butterfly shape. Cut on the line through both thicknesses.

Unfold the outside part of the paper and use the butterfly shape for some other project or use for scrap paper. Lay the cut paper over the dry watercolor painting, matching the edges. Glue or staple the two sheets of paper together.

Use black or brown crayons or markers to make antennae. Butterflies need two lines from the head. Moths should have two lines plus small crosslines for their antennae.

23

DRAGON EGG CARTON

Materials Needed

- One bumpy half of an egg carton per dragon
- One paper cup for each dragon head
- Scraps of red and green construction paper and/or other colors

- Green tempera paint
- Paintbrushes
- Glue, staples, or brads
- Scissors
- Pencils

Paint the outside of the egg carton green. If the cup isn't green, the children may want to paint it green.

When the paint is dry, attach the cup to one end of the egg carton with glue, staples, or brads.

Cut a long, narrow triangle from red paper and glue to the head for a tongue.

Cut eyes from colored paper and glue to the head above the tongue.

Spine plates can be added by cutting triangles from green paper (or other colors). Fold under 1/4 inch of the shortest edge and glue the folded part to the top of a hump. One can be added to each hump.

Cut a 1 inch strip of green paper as long as you want the tail. Curl one end by wrapping it tightly around a pencil; then pull. Glue the uncurled end to the tail end of the dragon.

Pieces of green paper can be glued to the bottom of the carton for feet. The number of feet is optional.

STUFFED BAG TURKEY

Use crumpled newspapers to stuff the lunch bag well.

Close the end and fold over 1/2 inch and staple shut.

Select colored rectangles for the tail. Round off one end of each rectangle to make a feather shape.

Glue the feathers to the unstapled rectangular end of the bag.

Use crayons or markers to color in an eye, the beak, and wattles. Do both sides of the head.

Glue the head (can be a single piece of brown paper or can be cut from folded paper with the fold at the top of the head) to the stapled end of the bag, covering the staples if possible.

COLORFUL BIRDS, BUTTERFLIES, OR FISH

Materials Needed

- Two 9" x 10" or 2" x 5" sheets of wax paper
- Various colors of 1" square sheets of blue, green, or black tissue paper
- A 9" x 12" or 12" x 18" sheet of blue, green, or black construction paper.
- A mixture of liquid starch and white glue
- Brushes
- Glue or staples

Place one sheet of wax paper on a protected surface.

Paint the wax paper with the glue/starch mixture.

Lay pieces of colored tissue on the glue in the colors desired. Overlap colors slightly or lay them close together.

Paint the tissue with the glue/starch mixture gently.

Add more tissue to cover any holes as needed.

Be sure to thoroughly wash brushes immediately after using so the glue won't dry on them.

Fold the sheet of construction paper in half and cut a bird, butterfly, or fish shape through both thicknesses. Open the construction paper, place on tissue paper collage, and you'll see a brightly colored animal in the negative space.

Staple or glue the edges together, being sure to secure the wax paper in place with the glue or staples.

construction paper with negative cut out showing through

Alternative method: If you don't want to mess with glue but are comfortable supervising a reasonably warm iron, try this way:

Materials Needed

- same as 1, 3, and 6 as on previous page.
- Old pieces of crayons grated on a food grater. Keep the colors separate.
- An iron with controlled settings
- Pads of paper or other heat resistant surfaces on which to iron and set the iron while it is not in use
- An old cloth or piece of butcher paper larger than the wax paper

Have the children place a sheet of waxed paper on the paper pad.

Let them sprinkle the wax paper with their choice of colors of grated crayons. Keep them toward the center.

Lay the other piece of wax paper over the grated crayon.

Put the cloth or butcher paper over the wax paper.

Iron the cloth or paper slowly to melt the crayon crumbs.

A medium temperature of the iron will do. Supervise the children's handling of the iron closely.

When the melted crayon is cooled, place the precut folded paper on top and glue or staple together.

ELEPHANT

Materials Needed

- One box per child
- Newsprint
- Paint – in gray or pink, etc.
- Black paint or black markers
- Scraps of construction paper
- Glue
- Two buttons per elephant

Cover the boxes with newsprint using glue. (You may wish to do this step for very young children.) Let the glue and paper dry.

Paint the box. gray or pink. When dry, use the black paint or markers to paint the feet at the lower edge of the box.

Cut or tear ears, trunk, and tail from scraps of paper. Attach with glue. Glue on buttons for eyes.

Let the children display in an elephant parade – especially good if you've been talking about the circus.

DEER HAND PUPPET

Materials Needed

- One sheet per child of 8" x 10" brown construction paper
- Pencil
- Scissors
- One brown paper lunch bag per child
- Scraps of red, black, and white construction paper
- Glue or paste

The child or an adult (depending on the child's ability) draws around each hand on the brown paper. The fingers should be spread far apart.

Cut out the hands.

With the lunch bag closed and the bottom of the bag folded back on the underneath side, glue the hand shapes to the top of the bag. Make sure the fingers and thumbs extend above the bag.

From white paper, cut a 1" x 3" strip to glue down the center of the back of the sack from the top down.

Cut small white dots and glue them to the back of the bag on either side of the white strip for the spots of the fawn.

Carefully turn the sack over. From scraps, cut out a red nose and glue to the center bottom of the flap but not to the sack under the flap. Add eyes above the nose.

Use as a puppet over the hand with fingers bent into the flap to make the head move.

FRAMED ANIMAL PICTURE

The children select an animal picture from old magazines, etc., and cut it out. (It must be small enough to fit on the trays available.)

Trim the edges so the picture will fit on the flat part of the tray with a small margin or more.

Glue the picture to the tray.

Apply glue in a 1/2 inch to 2 inch band around the picture without covering any of the animal or extending it up the edge of the tray.

Press Easter basket grass onto the glue. Let the glue dry.

When the glue is dry, use the scissors to trim away any grass that extends beyond the outside edge of the tray. Also, trim the inside edge of the grass to an even oval, rectangle, or square – whatever fits the animal picture.

VALENTINE GIRAFFE

Materials Needed

- Three strips of pink construction paper 1 1/2" x 6" per child
- Numerous strips of red construction paper
- Red or black yarn
- Scraps (to cut eyes)
- Scissors
- Glue or paste
- A 9" x 12" sheet of background paper (optional – for mounting)

Glue one 6 inch pink strip to the bottom of another to form a right angle.

Fold the third strip in half lengthwise. Have the child place his/her thumb over the folded edge near the top and draw around it. Cut on the line made through both thicknesses, unfold, and he/she should have a heart shape to glue on the top of the giraffe neck for the head.

From the rest of the pink strip, cut four long legs and two short horns.

Glue the horns and legs in place.

Cut eyes from scraps and glue on the head.

Cut a length of yarn. Pull the threads apart on one end in a frayed manner. Glue on the body for a tail.

Fold a red strip in half lengthwise. Draw several hearts as shown for the head. Cut out and glue on the neck and body of the giraffe for the spots. Use more strips of red if needed for spots.

Glue the giraffe to a background or card if desired. A message might be, "I'll stick my neck out for you." Or, let children compose their own messages.

YARN ANIMAL SHAPES MOBILE

Materials Needed

- Lengths of yarn (not over about 12 - 14 inches long)
- Pictures or templates of animals
- Liquid starch mixed with glue (half & half)
- Craft sticks
- A stick, a coat hanger, or a wire loop and a piece of yarn or string for hanging
- Clear fishing line for hanging the mobile shapes
- Plastic bags

The child places his/her picture in the plastic bag flat and puts it on a protected surface. Tape each child's name on a corner or the back of his/her plastic bag.

Dip the appropriate color yarn (gray/whale, green/frog, brown or white/rabbit, pink/flamingo) in the starch/glue mixture and hold until it stops dripping.

Use the yarn to outline the animal shape in the plastic bag. Use another length of yarn to complete the outline if necessary, making sure the yarn overlaps and meets securely. Press the ends together. Cut off the excess yarn.

Let the children make other animals – the same or different – until they have enough for their mobile. Allow all shapes to dry.

Carefully remove the dried yarn from the plastic. Make sure it is **completely** dry.

Attach a length of clear fishing line or string to the top of the yarn animal shape and the other end to the hanger until all the shapes are attached. The animals can be hung at the same length or varying lengths.

CHINESE DRAGON

Materials Needed

- An old sheet or two long pieces of cloth
- Cloth scraps
- Safety pins
- A dragon mask or head
- Scissors
- A long, sacklike bag for the tail
- Newspapers for stuffing
- A small rope about 6 feet long

Green, brown, or gray are top color choices for the sheets/cloth, but even prints can be used. The width of the sheet depends on the height of the children. (Their feet and part of their legs should show when the sheet is over their heads widthwise.)

Arrange the children in a line with the tallest children in the middle. The smallest children should be toward the tail or head with the exception of the one who wears the mask. Use a paper bag to paint, glue paper to, or otherwise decorate for a dragon head. Make eyeholes for clear viewing. Children may have to take turns wearing the mask.

Secure the mask to the head of the first child. Pin or otherwise fasten the top of the sheet around his/her shoulders. You can pin the front together to just below the waist if you wish.

The other children in line place their hands firmly on the waist of the person in front of them and keep them there when the dragon is moving.

Drape the sheet over the heads of the line of children.

Tie the tail to the waist of the last child so that it follows far enough behind that he/she won't stumble over it.

Pin the middle of the end of the sheet to the rope tied to the end of the tail.

The dragon is ready to move forward and around in a parade.

STYROFOAM CATERPILLAR

Materials Needed

- Green construction paper (6" x 6" or 9" x 12") per child
- Scissors (optional)
- Hole punch
- Quantities of the worm-shaped styrofoam packing
- Glue

The child cuts a large leaf shape from the green construction paper if it is not precut.

The child uses the hole punch to make holes in the leaves where the caterpillar has eaten. If time permits, have each child tell how many caterpillars he/she wants and let him/her count them out.

Attach caterpillars to the leaf with small amounts of glue. Let them dry before handling.

CRAYON RESIST SWAN

Materials Needed

- One sheet of 12" x 18" white construction paper per child
- Crayons (pencil optional)
- Newspaper (for padding under the crayon coloring activity)
- Watercolors
- Watercolor brushes
- Sponge
- Containers to hold water for cleaning brushes

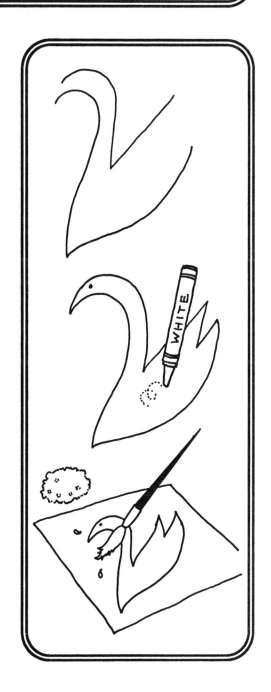

Use a black crayon to draw one or two swans. Begin by drawing a large number "2" with a long downward stroke and a bottom line that turns up slightly at the end.

Beginning at the start of the "2," draw a second "2" above the first "2" that gets further away until it's a little over halfway down what will be the swan's neck. Curve sharply upward for the tail of the swan. Connect the two lines with a slanted "M."

Draw a line marking off the top of the bill, and put in one eye.

Draw a second swan if you wish and if you have the room. It can be larger or smaller.

Place the drawing on a pad of paper. Let the children color the swan firmly with black or white with beak and eye of appropriate color. Fill in the shape with color.

Place the picture on a protected surface. Wet the blue and/or green color pans with two drops of water.

Use a sponge to wet the entire surface of the picture, or dip the picture in a pan or sink of water.

Use the blue and/or green watercolors to paint the surface around the swans.

Let it dry.

CARP KITE OR A STUFFED FISH

Materials Needed

- A sheet of classified newspaper per child 22" x 28", newsprint, or a sheet of butcher paper*
- Crayons or felt-tip markers of many colors
- Scissors
- Glue
- String or wire to fit around

the mouth edge and string to fly the kite if you aren't stuffing it
- Tape
- Quantities of newspaper for stuffing (optional)
- A stick or dowel 3 to 6 feet long (optional)

Fold the newspaper in half and cut in a fish shape without cutting the folded edge. (An adult can draw the fish shape on the folded paper and let the child cut it out.) Remember that fish come in countless sizes and shapes, so with a tail, a body, and a mouth, you can hardly miss.

Open the cut shape and lay it flat. Let the children decorate it with crayons or felt-tip markers. Fold back 1/2 inch on the mouth edge two times and glue the edge in place. Tape a string or wire around the mouth edge leaving ends of string hanging out.

*Butcher paper is heavier and may not fly well. It's better for making a stuffed fish.

Fold the fish back together and glue the bottom edges leaving the mouth and tail open.

When the glue is dry, shape the mouth edge into a circle.

Fasten kite string to the mouth edge and fly the kite.

The children can fly with a string, or you may find it better to fasten a short string to the carp and fasten the other end of the string to the top of a stick or dowel so the children can hold the stick and run with it to fly the fish.

DRAWING SQUIRRELS

Materials Needed

- One sheet of paper per child
- A pencil or crayon per child

Guide the children through the first squirrel drawing by demonstrating each step for them to do just before they do it.

Draw a large "S."

Make a large circle at the bottom end of the "S" for a fat body.

Draw another "S" beside the first; "attach" the bottom to the large circle.

Put a smaller circle on the top of the large circle for a head.

Put two eyes on the head about halfway down from the top of the circle.

Add a small round nose below the eyes with two lines making an upside-down "V" below the nose but touching it. Make two larger upside-down "Vs" for ears at the top of the head.

At the bottom of the large circle opposite the large "S," put an oval shape for the foot.

Put a shorter oval shape for another foot on the same side of the body but closer to the head.

To make a bushy tail, draw lines across the large "S." The more lines they draw, the bushier the tail, and the longer the lines, the bigger the tail.

40

DRAWING PIGS

Materials Needed

- One sheet of paper per child
- A pencil or crayon per child

Guide the children through drawing their first pig by demonstrating one step at a time and giving them time to follow each direction before moving to the next step. Then encourage them to make more pigs.

Draw a large circle.

Put a circle inside that circle about half as big.

Put one small circle inside the smaller circle and color or pencil in two dots. This is the snout.

Place two circles above the snout for eyes. Make a dot for a dark pupil in each eye.

Put two upside-down "Vs" on the second circle for ears.

Under the large circle, place two rectangles for legs and feet. (Remind children that pigs don't have long legs.)

On the top of the large circle, draw a line with a loop in it for a tail.

Encourage children to make a field full of pigs so they can master the process and include big and little pigs.

You may have to repeat the guiding steps for those less confident.

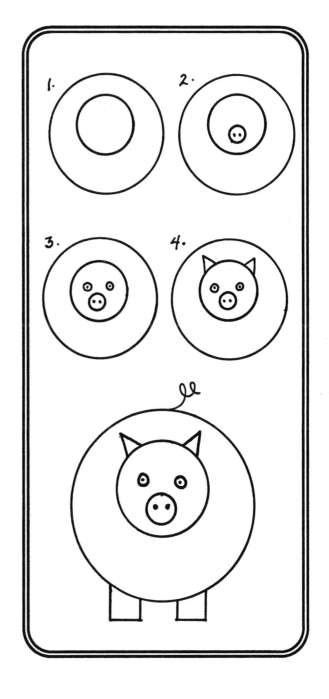

Note: This activity and the preceding one, "Drawing Squirrels," can be fun to do and give a child confidence that he/she can draw.

41

RABBIT

Materials Needed

- One juice can, oatmeal box, or cylinder of paper* per child
- Paint in white, brown, or pink
- Paintbrushes
- Ears, eyes, nose, mouth, and whiskers**
- Glue or paste
- Scissors

Let the children paint the box or can in the color of their choice. Let it dry.

The children cut or tear and attach ears, eyes, nose, whiskers, and mouth to the cylinder. Have a model to observe, or direct the activity beginning with the ears at the top of the cylinder. They should place the eyes halfway down the cylinder. Then add the nose and mouth.

Attach the whiskers last, putting them between the nose and mouth.

*If paper cylinders are used, the painting process can be eliminated.

**These can be precut, or let the children cut or tear their own shapes from scraps.

SNAIL

Materials Needed

- Two paper plates per child
- One strip of brown or beige paper 1 1/2" x 4" and another strip 1/2" x 2" per child
- Crayons
- Glue
- Scissors
- Containers of water
- Cotton balls
- Tempera paint in green, brown, or pink
- Paintbrushes (optional)

Place small quantities of the paint in small containers such as jar lids. The child can paint the back of each plate, using the same color on both plates. If white plates are used and the child desires a white snail, there is no need to paint. Use brushes or fingers to rub the paint around.

The child cuts a rounded head shape out of one end of the longer strip of paper. He/she cuts a pointed tail shape on one end of the shorter paper. You may wish to predraw a line to cut.

Using crayons, draw eyes on each side of the head.

Put glue on the concave side of both paper plates.

Place the uncut end of the head inside the lower edge of the plate. On the other side of the plate, place the uncut end of the tail inside the lower edge of the plate, being sure the head and tail extend over the outside edge of the plate.

Place the other plate over the one with the head and tail being sure the edges match. Press the edges together securely all around.

Draw a shell shape spiral on both sides of the plates beginning each spiral just above the top of the head, or start in the center and end the outer spiral at the top of the head.

Dampen the plate surface slightly. Dip cotton balls in the tempera paint and rub on the plate for color if not previously painted.

TURTLES

Materials Needed

- One 3" x 18" strip of green or brown tagboard for each child
- Two strips of green or brown construction paper 1 1/2" x 7" per child
- Scraps for tail and eyes

- Glue
- Scissors
- Stapler
- Felt-tip markers or red or yellow sequins (optional)

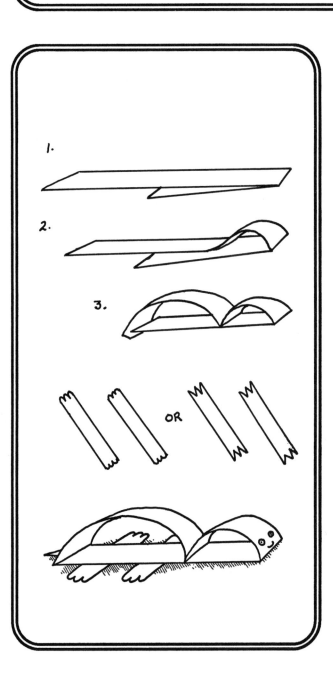

1.

2.

3.

OR

Lightly mark a folding line 6 or 6 1/2" from one end of the tagboard.

Have the children fold the 3" x 18" strip on the marked folding line.

Holding the folded paper with the short end on the bottom, push up the top strip to form a head about 1 1/2 inches high. Staple the top piece to the bottom piece about 1 1/2 inches from the fold, forming the head of the turtle.

Fold under 1/2 inch at the end of the remaining strip. Place it next to the head of the turtle and glue or staple in place.

Cut toe shapes on the ends of each 1 1/2" x 7" strip. Show rounded or sharp toe options.

Glue the feet strips to the bottom of the turtle body (not under the head).

Glue on a cut or torn scrap for a tail. Use other scraps for eyes. You can add eyes with felt-tip markers or red or yellow sequins.

Spots and/or lines can be added to the body with scraps.

PAPER DOUGH

Ingredients

- Paper/newspaper scraps torn into small pieces
- 1 quart of water
- 1 teaspoon salt
- Wallpaper paste

Put paper scraps to soak in one quart of water in which the salt has been dissolved. Let it stand for 36 hours.

Mix the paper into a pulp (squeezing it with the hands is one way), and add the wallpaper paste until you have a molding consistency. Mold into a shape.

When this dries, it is hard. Paint as desired.

CREPE PAPER DOUGH

This recipe makes about one cup of dough, so multiply accordingly. Torn pieces may not mat together as much as cut pieces when it comes to mixing.

Materials Needed

- 1 1/2 cups of torn or cut crepe paper packed in a cup
- 1 1/2 cups of water
- 1/2 cup of flour

Soak the crepe paper overnight.

Pour off any excess water.

Mix in the flour and knead to the desired consistency.

This is a good medium for precolored animals such as yellow for canaries, ducks, or cats from tabbies to tigers; green for frogs, lizards, or dinosaurs; etc. All you have to add is eyes, stripes, spots, or other features with colored markers or paint.

SOAK

MIX

KNEAD

PRETZEL ANIMALS

This dough can be eaten.

Yeast doughs such as this one and the one that follows work better with some different molding techniques than the other clays or doughs. Because of the elasticity of the dough, using a dull knife to cut legs, tail, tusks, or arms from a larger mass and moving them into place seems to work better than pulling or pinching out appendages. Pinching pieces together may not adhere well after baking and may fall off if handled too much. Smaller item such as ears, horns, or toes can usually be pinched out successfully. Raisins can be used for eyes.

Ingredients

- 1 package of yeast
- 4 cups of flour
- 1 1/2 cups of warm water
- 1 tablespoon sugar
- 1 tablespoon salt
- 1 egg

Use a large bowl in which to mix the yeast in warm water with the sugar and the salt.

Stir in the flour.

Knead on a floured surface until the mixture is smooth.

Shape into animals such as snakes, an octopus, fish, crabs, bear, giraffe, whale, earthworms, snails, spiders, birds, etc.

Place on a baking sheet.

Brush each animal with the beaten egg.

Bake in an oven at 425° for 15 minutes or until browned.

This is edible. To keep permanently, shellac the animal after it has cooled and is dry.

DOUGH TO EAT

Ingredients

- 1 package of dry yeast
- 1 1/2 cups of warm water
- 1 egg
- 1/4 cup of honey
- 1/4 cup of cooking oil
- 1 teaspoon salt
- 5 cups of flour

Place the yeast in warm water and stir it until it dissolves.

Add the egg, honey, oil, and salt. Stir.

Add as much of the flour as needed to make it easy to handle.

Knead for 5 minutes, adding flour as it gets sticky. This is a job for the children perhaps.

Shape the figures of animals, and carefully place on a cookie sheet. A metal spatula may help. The animals can be as large or as small as desired, but they should be kept relatively flat. Fat, rounded shapes tend to lose their features when the dough rises.

Cover the animals on the cookie sheet with a cloth and set in a warm place.

Let the dough rise for 25 minutes or more.

Remove the cloth and bake for 20 minutes at 350° or until golden brown in color.

The animals may be eaten when cool and dry. Or they may be shellacked to be kept permanently.

GINGERBREAD

Ingredients

- Mix 1/2 cup oil
  1 cup brown sugar
  1 1/2 cups molasses
- Stir in 2/3 cup cold water
- Sift together and stir in:
  7 cups flour

2 teaspoons soda
1 teaspoon salt
1 teaspoon ginger
1 teaspoon cloves
1 teaspoon cinnamon

Chill the dough.

Roll out part of the dough 1/2" thick.

Use a dull knife to cut into animal shapes, use cookie cutters of animal shapes, or mold into animal shapes with the hands and flatten to 1/2 inch thickness. Remember that a gingerbread boy is an animal, too.

You can add raisins for eyes.

Place on a baking sheet.

Bake at 350° for 15 minutes. Let them cool some before removing them from the cookie sheet.

SAWDUST CLAY

This clay is **not** edible.

Add water to get the workable dough a consistency that pleases you. Mold into animal shapes – anything from lizards to elephants.

It should harden overnight.

If desired, paint when dry.

Sawdust Clay

Mix 6 cups dry sawdust with 5 1/2 cups flour and 2 tablespoons salt.

Carefully add small amounts of boiling water until you get a stiff dough.

This dough needs lots of kneading and requires additional amounts of sawdust to get the consistency you want. Use as soon as it is cool enough, or store in an airtight container in a cool place.

This recipe makes a large amount – perhaps more than other dough recipes. It's a great medium for large objects with simple lines.

Aged sawdust (one or two years old) turns a dark gray color. New sawdust is more brown. (Carpenters and construction sites are sources of free sawdust, as are sawmills and possibly building supply stores.)

TOOLS AND TECHNIQUES FOR DOUGHS AND CLAYS

Some tools for dough and clay animals are:
- rolling pins
- cookie cutters
- plastic spoons, knives, and forks
- craft sticks
- garlic press to make hair or fur
- hands

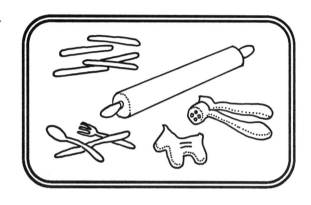

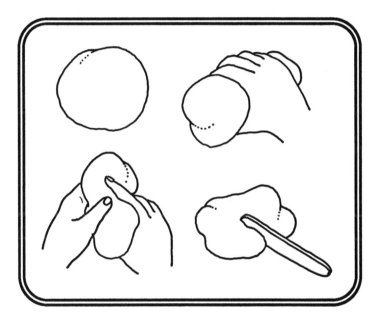

Forming an animal – shape the dough or clay into a ball.

Pull or squeeze out part of the ball into a pear or mushroom shape.

Holding the large end in your hand, use a finger or two of the other hand to rock back and forth crosswise through the center of the large end forming legs.

Use a craft stick to cut the legs apart to make 4 legs and to cut a mouth.

Add further features by pulling out feet, ears, tail, etc., as desired.

Use a pencil point to make eyes.

If the animal is fat and will be baked or fired, form a hole in the underside of the abdomen (or the bottom if it is a sitting figure) to keep it from exploding.

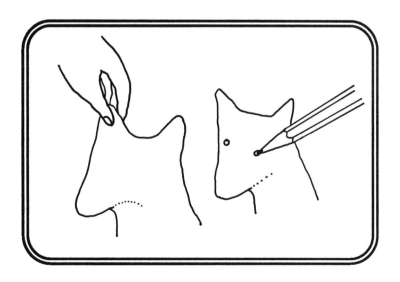

CARVING ANIMALS

Materials Needed

- Something to carve
  A. Styrofoam chunks (messy, but easily available from packing)
  B. Soap
  C. Cork
  D. Blocks of wax
  E. Make your own blocks to carve by mixing equal amounts of plaster of Paris and vermiculite and pouring into an empty milk carton. Let it harden and dry before carving.
  F. Mix equal amounts of plaster of Paris and sawdust and pour into empty milk cartons to harden and dry before carving.
- Tools to carve with: nails, not-so-sharp knives, spoons, scissors, sharp sticks, or hammer and chisel.

This is a good project for outdoors where cleanup may be easier. Otherwise, work on an easily swept surface or use a dropcloth on the floor.

The children take the medium to be carved and an available tool and work to shape a whale, sitting duck, dolphin, bear, elephant, or any animal without too many appendages, particularly long, thin ones.

A picture of the animal desired can be taped to one side of the chunk used to guide the children in getting started. (The picture can be removed when it gets in the way.)

AN OWL TO CUT

Materials Needed

- One 9" x 12" sheet of brown construction paper per owl
- Two 3" x 3" pieces of yellow or orange construction paper per owl
- Two black and two larger white circles for the eyes per owl
- One orange triangle beak
- Scissors
- Glue or paste

Cut out the body from the 9" x 12" sheet, folded in half crosswise with a half owl shape drawn on it. (See illustration.) Open it flat.

Cut out the feet from folded yellow or orange paper. Open them flat and glue the straight edges to the bottom of the owl.

Cut out the eyes if not precut. The eyes can also be cut from folded paper with the semicircles drawn against the fold. Glue the large white circles to the upper part of the owl. Glue the smaller circles on the white circles.

The owls can be put on a fall or Halloween bulletin board if you cut the trunk and bare branches of a tree, fasten the tree to the bulletin board, and perch the owls on the limbs. Add a moon, cats, witches, bats – whatever you wish.

PRETZEL AND COOKIE OWLS

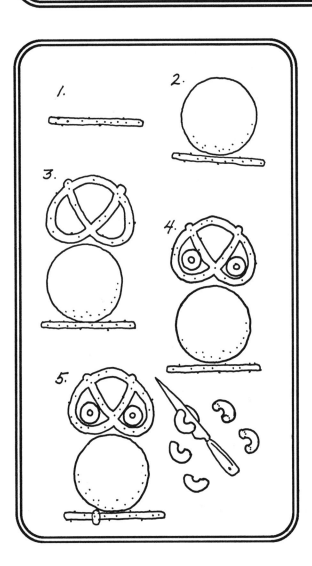

If you use burlap and the edges will be fringed, then pull some threads on three sides of the material. The fourth side is the top to be fastened to a stick or piece of wood.

Add glue to one side of a straight pretzel. Press the glued side gently to the background wherever the owl will sit.

Apply glue to the back of a cookie. Set the cookie on top of the straight pretzel and press gently.

Apply glue to one side of the twisted pretzel. Place it above the cookie, but touching, with the straighter edge at the top.

Apply glue to two unbroken cereal pieces. Press one gently into each circle in the twisted pretzel for eyes.

Using fingernails or some cutting instrument, break two or three cereal pieces in half.

Place glue on the inside curved edge. Gently press the half cereal piece over the straight pretzel under the owl body. Use two or three halves placed close together for each of the two owl's feet.

Repeat for more owls in your picture, if you wish.

Add moon, trees, branches, fences, etc., as desired.

When the glue has dried thoroughly, staple or glue the top of the cloth to a stick of wood so that the wood extends a 1/2 inch or more beyond the cloth on both sides.

When the glue has dried, tie each end of a length of yarn, etc., to each end of the piece of wood as a hanger.

*Fabric can be broadcloth, burlap, or any plain or small printed cloth. Or, use a paper plate, heavy cardboard, wood, tagboard, etc. This is used to glue the owl. If you use burlap, the side and edges can be fringed by pulling out threads at the edge for 1/4 to 1/2 inch.

ZEBRA PATTERN

TIGER PATTERN

CAT PATTERN

DOG PATTERN

BAT PATTERN/ BUTTERFLY PATTERN

TURKEY PATTERN

BIRD PATTERNS

FISH PATTERN